How to Get Things Done Without Trying Too Hard

Prentice Hall LIFE

If life is what you make it, then making it better starts here.

What we learn today can change our lives tomorrow. It can change our goals or change our minds; open up new opportunities or simply inspire us to make a difference. That's why we have created a new breed of books that do more to help you make more of *your* life.

Whether you want more confidence or less stress, a new skill or a different perspective, we've designed *Prentice Hall Life* books to help you to make a change for the better. Together with our authors we share a commitment to bring you the brightest ideas and best ways to manage your life, work and wealth.

In these pages we hope you'll find the ideas you need for the life *you* want. Go on, help yourself.

It's what you make it

* * *

How to Get Things Done Without Trying Too Hard

RICHARD TEMPLAR

Harlow, England • London • New York • Boston • San Francisco • Toronto • Sydney • Singapore • Hong Kong
Tokyo • Seoul • Taipei • New Delhi • Cape Town • Madrid • Mexico City • Amsterdam • Munich • Paris • Milan

PEARSON EDUCATION LIMITED

Edinburgh Gate
Harlow CM20 2JE
Tel: +44 (0)1279 623623
Fax: +44 (0)1279 431059
Website: www.pearsoned.co.uk

First published in Great Britain in 2009

ISBN: 978-0-273-72556-5

British Library Cataloguing-in-Publication Data
A catalogue record for this book is available from the British Library

Library of Congress Cataloging-in-Publication Data
A catalogue record for this book is available from the Library of Congress

10 9 8 7 6 5 4 3 2 1
13 12 11 10 09

Text design by Design Deluxe
Typeset in ClassicalGaramondBT-Roman by 30
Printed and bound in Great Britain by Clays Ltd, Bungay, Suffolk

The publisher's policy is to use paper manufactured from sustainable forests.

For my brilliant editor and even more brilliant friend Rachael, without whom I would get far less done

Contents

Introduction

I'm guessing since you've picked up this book that you think that you don't get as much done as you could. Maybe stuff is always falling off the edges or you just can't seem to deal with everything that needs dealing with. It could be that you feel locked in a never-ending struggle to do everything well and on time, but no matter how hard you try, it never seems to happen. Perhaps you look at other people, with their charmed lives of order and effortless accomplishment, and wonder why you can't be like that – and put it down to just not being one of life's naturally organised people.

Well, I'll let you into a secret. No one is. All those people you know who seem to you to get loads done don't have any innate gift for remembering dates, keeping on top of their home life or prioritising their work. They just know techniques and strategies that you don't. In fact, some of the most organised people you know – the ones who always remember your birthday – secretly have the most dreadful memories. That's why they've had no choice but to train themselves up or they'd never manage to do what they do.

Some of the skills you need are purely practical. I've included the most important of these in this book because you won't get much done without them. A lot of the work, however, needs to happen inside your head. Your mental approach to chores, to-do lists or a bulging in-tray is the most important thing of all.

Over the years I've watched the people who seem to achieve most in life – the ones who hold down a full-time job while bringing up a family, looking after an elderly parent or two, doing some charity work on the side, and keeping the garden looking perfect. Some of them look as if they're not even breaking a sweat. It's effortless, easy, smooth.

These people know something the rest of us don't. They know how to approach a huge workload without panicking, how to stay cheerful while they work through it, and how to wake up the next morning and do it all again without feeling resentful or frustrated or miserable. And what I've realised is that the reason for this is that they have so many strategies under their belt they really don't have to try too hard.

It sounds so simple, doesn't it? In fact, it sounds implausibly, unrealistically, improbably simple. But yes, that's really all there is to it.

Of course, it takes practice to use all these skills without having to think about them. And you need the right attitude. That's what this book is all about. I wanted to pass on the tips I've learned from other people over the years, the observations I've made about their attitude to getting things done, and the practical strategies they use.

You'll probably find it hard work incorporating all of these into your life simultaneously. So have a look through and pick out the most promising-looking ones to start with. Maybe the easiest ones, or perhaps the ones you need most. Once you've incorporated them into your life, add the next few, and the next. Before long you'll find you're getting far more done than you were before, and that you're making no more effort than you were. In fact, you'll find that life is easier than before.

Before you start, of course, you do have to show commitment. So put reading this book – and acting on it – at the top of your to-do list, and make sure you get it done.

I'm always interested to pick up more tips, so if you have any thoughts or ideas feel free to email me at **Richard.Templar@RichardTemplar.com**.

Richard Templar

You can and you can't

It was Henry Ford, I believe, who said, "Whether you think you can or whether you think you can't, you're probably right."

In other words if you look at the pile of things you have to do and your heart sinks and you think, "I'll never get through this", you probably won't. On the other hand, if you think, "This could take a while. Best get cracking ..." you'll almost certainly get it all done.

You're no different from anyone else. Think of the person you know with the busiest life who still manages to fit everything in. You know, the ones who even remember to bring you a personally chosen gift or a bunch of flowers from their garden when they come over for a meal.

Well, if they can do it, so can you. And you absolutely have to believe this. Or be open to the possibility at the very least. Every time you start to flag, look at them and remind yourself that it's possible. Getting things done really is all in the mind, and once you realise that you have the same raw materials as everyone else – a brain, a pair of hands and so on – you'll realise that once you acquire the skills you can match anyone for getting things done effortlessly.

YOU HAVE TO WANT
TO BE ORGANISED

Most of us would prefer to be organised, at least in some ways. We might quite enjoy our haphazard approach to cooking, but wish we could reliably find our car keys every time we need them. Maybe we like our holidays to be a series of surprises, but we'd love our meetings to run on time.

If you want to become more organised it doesn't take effort, but it does take commitment. If you just fancy the idea of being organised, it's probably not going to work. You need to really want to be a more organised person, deep in your heart, if you're going to make any real difference to your life.

If that's truly what you want, it's really not hard. It's the wanting it that's the tricky bit. So if you haven't quite reached that stage, spend a week or two being brutally honest with yourself every time your life is more stressful than it need be because you were less organised than you could have been. Did you panic when you thought you'd lost your ticket? Have to rush to an appointment because you were frantically finishing something off? Forced to spend ages sorting through a pile of papers to find something, getting more and more frustrated, and all because you had let it build up and up for months instead of dealing with it as it came in? Did you feel terrible when you realised you'd missed that important person's birthday again, for the fifth year running?

Once you've realised how much stress you could shed if you were better organised, you may be ready to commit yourself to doing something about it.

You don't have to change your personality

If you have an image of yourself as an unorganised person, you may be reluctant to lose it. Of course you don't tell yourself you're unorganised. You'll think of yourself as spontaneous or ditsy or freedom-loving or charmingly forgetful. And you'll probably think of organised people as being boring, staid, grown-up, passionless and predictable. This, despite the fact that you probably have loads of organised friends and family who are none of these things but can still catch a train without rushing for it.

Look, I know how it feels. I don't like the idea of being an organised person either. It doesn't suit my self-image. If I'm entirely honest with myself, I am quite organised. I don't see myself that way because I've learned lots of ways of getting things done over the years, but all I've changed is my behaviour. Underneath I'm not an organised person at all. I'm still the same exciting, spontaneous, take-it-as-it-comes sort of person I always was.[1] It's just that now I make lists and remember where I left my glasses.

So don't worry. You don't have to turn into one of those tedious, soulless, organised people. You can still be fun and frivolous and live in the moment. It's just that you'll be efficient and organised with it, even if you are only pretending.

---

[1] At least that's what I like to think I always was.

Know yourself

My life is always busy, and there's always a to-do list that doesn't get finished. I used to think that if I could just change this, or change that, everything would clear and I'd be able to relax. But it's never happened.

Funnily enough, it's only by watching other people go through this that I've realised what the problem is. And I've realised that it isn't a problem. You see, I actually *like* being busy all the time. Every time I manage to free up a chunk of time, what do I do? Take up golf, or spend more time reading, or sit around drinking coffee? Of course not. I just find something else to fill the time with. Because, deep down, that's how I like it.

So if your life is always a mad rush, think about whether that's actually what you want and, if so, stop fretting. What you need to consider is quality of life. I've been through phases where I didn't even have time to clean my teeth or get the shopping done, and that's just silly. But so long as I'm busy with things I enjoy doing, at least most of the time, I've stopped fretting. I've come to recognise that I can't change that, and I wouldn't be happy if I did.

If you're this kind of person, you'll find loads of strategies in this book that will ensure that the things that need doing get done, and you'll free up enough time to fill with busy things you enjoy doing. But don't expect to have loads of free time because, if you're honest, that's not what you really want. You'd only fill it with something else, because that's what actually makes you happy.

MAKE TIME

The greatest obstacle to efficiency is lack of time. We could all remember everything given long enough. Given time, a chimpanzee could apparently type the complete works of Shakespeare, so surely we could clear our list of chores and tasks and jobs – eventually.

However, time is just what you don't have. So the first thing you need to do is know how to make time, whether you want to clear an extra half an hour a day to take the pressure off, or whether you want to find a whole day or two for a particular project.

To begin with, look for things that could be done quicker. If you threw together a quick supper instead of cooking a delicious but long-winded recipe, you'd save at least half an hour. Or perhaps you could delegate something else at work. Or deal with that chatterbox by email instead of by phone. Or organise a lift-share for the school run. You can be constantly on the lookout for tasks you can speed up. And of course most of this book is designed to save you time too.

If you want to clear a chunk of time for a specific reason, my favourite technique is to imagine that some crisis has happened. If you're emotionally vulnerable you don't have to make this anything tragic. Suppose there's a power cut and you can't use your computer for 24 hours. How would you cope? Whatever the answer is, do it anyway without the power cut. Or suppose your father was rushed to hospital,[2] and you had to take 24 hours out to be with your mum? You see, you'll always find the time if it's essential, so just pretend it is. And then get right on with whatever it is that you desperately needed the time for.

[2] It's OK, it turns out fine.

HAVE A ROUTINE

I used to hate routine. Of course I had a very loose routine – I mostly slept at night and generally ate three meals at variable points during the day. But compared with a lot of people I had the luxury of working from home. As long as I made my deadlines it was up to me what time of day, and indeed what days of the week, I worked.

When my eldest child was born, I was flung into a parallel universe where it was almost impossible to get anything done. Even organising a meal could be hard going, by the time I'd dealt with work and a baby who never slept. My wife was in exactly the same situation, and we decided to inject just a little bit of routine into the day. We'd make sure that we took it in turns to look after the baby for a set few hours each morning.

It was like flicking a switch. Instantly life started to become manageable. It wasn't easy, though, so we tentatively added a bit more routine. Wham! Things became clearer still. And we made a discovery – when you're really busy, the more of a routine you have, the easier your life becomes. Having minimal routines is great when you're a student, or once you retire, but if you have a busy life it's a luxury you can't afford.

So walk the dog at the same time every day, change the sheets on a Sunday morning, deal with correspondence on a Monday afternoon, phone your mother straight after the TV news, check your emails when you get back from lunch. The more routine you build into your life, the less effort it will take to keep things on track. And no, it doesn't mean you are boring. If you think it does, just turn the page …

Don't tell yourself you're bored

Are you one of those people who thinks it's boring to be organised and effective and get things done? Boring to make lists or keep a diary or remember your nephew's birthday?

Well, I'm sorry, but that attitude just won't wash. Yes, some of those things may not sound scintillating, but I can promise you that there's a lot less boredom in an effectively run life than a disorganised one. Because, if you're good at getting things done, think of all the boredom you'll avoid, in exchange for keeping a proper diary and writing the odd list. Can you honestly tell me any of the following aren't boring?

- Spending an hour on a cold station platform because you missed your train.
- Spending hours on the phone to the electricity company stopping them cutting you off because you somehow forgot to pay the bill.
- Staying up to midnight to get your report ready for your boss in the morning because you didn't start it when you meant to.
- Hunting all over the house for ages for your passport because you don't know where you put it and you're off on holiday tomorrow.
- Pushing your way through heaving crowds trying to get all your Christmas shopping done the week before Christmas.

And I haven't even started yet. Right, let's hear no more about it being boring getting things done.

DON'T GET DISTRACTED

I don't know about you, but I find the Internet is the biggest culprit here. It's not generally a deliberate ploy on my part – rather it's just that I'm online for some legitimate reason and something catches my eye.

The only way to deal with this is to be upfront with yourself. Tell yourself, "I'm getting distracted and I don't have time for this now." Then make yourself a note (if necessary) so you can go back to whatever it was later. If it was the Internet, the odds are when you look at the note later you'll decide it's not worth the bother.

Of course it might have been something you genuinely needed to do. But that still doesn't mean now is the time to do it. The laundry does indeed need to be done, but not when you're in the middle of writing the shopping list. Wait until you've finished or you'll waste five minutes trying to remember where you were when you come back to the list. And just because your emails need doing, it's not worth interrupting your train of thought preparing for this afternoon's meeting. You can deal with your inbox later.

As with procrastinating, the point is to catch yourself red-handed. You know in the back of your mind that you're doing it. Bring it to the front of your mind and face it, and it's far easier to control.

THINK ABOUT
WHAT YOU'RE NOT
THINKING ABOUT

I love procrastinating. And though I say it myself, I'm very good at it. I can spend a whole morning making cups of tea and writing lists, rather than sitting down and getting on with my work. As a teenager – like most teenagers – I could spend so long perfecting my exam revision timetable that I couldn't possibly fit in the time to actually revise.

Of course, I only do this when there's something I should be getting on with and don't want to. Something I don't want to think about. Generally it's something difficult, at least in the sense that I haven't yet worked out how to go about it. Sometimes it involves a conversation I think might be tricky. Occasionally it involves something dirty and unappealing, like fixing the car or cleaning the oven.

Whatever it is, you need to learn to recognise the signs of procrastination. My hunch is that you already do recognise them. As soon as you catch yourself using these delaying tactics on yourself, you need to face up to whatever you're putting off and ask yourself why. Why do I not want to get on with this? Often a clear answer to this question is all you need to break the pattern. If that doesn't work, make yourself do it first and get it over with. You know you'll thank yourself for it later.

DON'T PANIC!

Sometimes the workload seems overwhelming. You don't know where to start and the scale of it all is just plain terrifying. Well, if looking at the big picture is too scary, don't look at it.

However you handle this, you can only do one thing at a time. You can do them fast and effectively and plough through them and tick them all off your list, but you can only do them one at a time.

So put your head down and only look at one corner of that wall of work. One room of the house, not the whole three floors. One thing on your desk, not every piece of paper on it. Start with something that's urgent, and then work your way through. Deal with the wall brick by brick. Don't think about the scale of it, and just plug away, bit by bit, until you feel you're making headway. When you finally look up, you'll be surprised to see how much of it you've dealt with.

Use the strategies in this book – and any others you know – to get each task done as effectively and swiftly as possible, and you'll find that once the panic subsides the work will somehow get done. It always does.

Do it little
and often

You know how easy it is for certain jobs to pile up and become overwhelming. It might be tidying or filing or keeping your diary up to date. If you're like me it could be all three of these and plenty more. The trick, as I've learned slowly and painfully, is to do these things little and often.

It's so little hassle to file a piece of paper as soon as you've read it, you don't even notice you're doing it. Similarly, if you update your diary every morning, it takes seconds. You can sidestep most tidying by putting things away in the right place to begin with (though getting the rest of the family to play ball can be harder).

These are habits you have to get into, which means that it's harder at the beginning. Within days, however, you start to appreciate the difference. So come on, what are the things that pile up for you? The ones you dread tackling because they get out of hand and then take ages? Well, those are the ones to practise this strategy on first, because that's where you'll really see the difference.

Think positive

If you're dealing with a mountain of work, you'll get through it far quicker if you're in a positive frame of mind. So focus on the things you've achieved so far, not on the ones still on your list.

Remember that the work always gets done in the end – or the world continues to go around without it. If it never gets done then obviously it wasn't essential. Because if it were essential, it would have been done.

I've known frantically busy people encounter the kind of crisis that means nothing gets done – a building burns down, or someone dies, or a business goes bust. The world still keeps spinning though. Keep everything in perspective and don't sweat over the minor stuff. So you haven't had time to shop today – I'm sure there's something in the cupboard and the kids won't starve. You didn't get through your emails and now there'll be even more tomorrow – maybe there will, but the important ones will get done. It may not be ideal but if you can't change things there's no point stressing over them.

So look on the bright side and think about what you *have* achieved. It will help you to see how much more you can do.

STEER CLEAR OF
TIME SAPPERS

Some things just eat up time. The most obvious one, as I've mentioned, is the Internet. I don't want to knock it because I know it's a brilliant invention, makes all our lives easier, etc. etc. but it can waste as much time as it saves if you let it.

We all have our own time sappers. Backgammon is one of mine. Once I start playing I don't know where the time goes. Electronic toys from PlayStations to Wii are common ones, and others don't involve playing at all. Some people spend hours in the kitchen, cooking things that taste delicious but take ages, when they're quite capable of whipping up something just as delicious in a fraction of the time. I know people who spend hours cleaning when frankly a quick vacuum round would have done the job. And then there are time sappers in people form – the ones who you simply can't have a quick chat with because it always turns into two hours or more, when you least have two hours to spare.

When you're not pressed for time, of course all these things are fine. But if you want to get more done you'll need to learn where your time goes and be firm about the time sappers. By far the best approach is to steer clear altogether. Save them for when your time isn't limited, and while you're busy give them a wide berth.

Know when the good times are

Everybody has their own most productive time of day. I've heard it's usually the same time of day you were born, though that seems most unlikely to me. And of no help to anyone who doesn't know when they were born. Personally, I've found my best time has changed over my lifetime.

I used to work best at about 2am, probably due to the peace and quiet. These days I'm at my most productive during the first half of the morning. You may be an afternoon person or an evening person. Or even a 5am person (boy, am I glad I'm not one of those, I hate getting up early).

You need to know when you're at your best so you can play to your strengths. Make sure you don't waste this part of the day, but spend it doing the things you most need to get done. That might mean working on something that takes a lot of concentration, or something you've been dreading, or maybe this is the time to get through a great chunk of your long to-do list at lightning speed. You can decide how to spend the time – just don't fritter it if you want to get things done.

DO THE
SCARY JOBS

If you put off the most daunting tasks until the last minute, odds are you'll get them done double quick. Few things are as effective as an inescapable deadline. However, this method has its disadvantages:

- If there isn't a firm deadline the job may hang over you indefinitely.
- You spend days or weeks with a sense of dread when you could have had a sense of achievement if you'd done the job sooner.
- You may not do the thing nearly as well as you could have when you're up against the clock.

I know you don't want to do this thing, but you're going to have to sooner or later. I'm sure if you could have got out of it you would have done. So think about how you'll feel this time tomorrow if: a) you've done it; or b) you haven't. Because that's the only choice you've got – one way or another you *will* have to do it. The only thing you can control is when.

I'm sure you can see that if you just get the wretched thing out of the way, you'll be so much happier. So go on – do it. Now.

Set
yourself
limits

No matter what you do for a living, there are different things you need to spend your time on. Even as a writer, where you'd have thought I do the same thing all day, this is the case. I don't just sit and write all the time. I plan new projects, write existing ones, deal with emails, deal with household admin and bills (far too many of those). Then there's the time I have to spend putting the laundry through, shopping, walking the dog and so on. All these are tasks which can be done at any time when nothing else specific is scheduled.

Whether you work or not, this will be the case. And one of the problems with getting things done is that many of these things can slip. You find you were too long at the shops, or it's half past three and you haven't dealt with your inbox yet, or you're not getting around to your writing because everything else is calling to you.[3]

The answer to this is to set yourself start and stop times. These have to be realistic because this isn't going to work unless you stick to them. For example, when I'm writing I allow myself until 9am to get everything I can done in the house – laundry, cleaning or whatever. Then I go to work and have from 9 to 10am to clear any urgent tasks, check my emails and so on. Then I start writing at 10am.

Only you know what timetable will work for you, but if you don't build in start and stop times, you won't get everything done.

[3] Who, me?

INVEST NOW, SAVE LATER

I know the point of this book is to get things done *without trying too hard*. But sometimes you need to put in a bit more work now in order to make things run more smoothly later.

How often do you find yourself thinking, "If only I'd done such and such, this would be so much quicker." Well, next time you think it, act on it. If you put a decent filing system in place it would indeed take you an hour or two, but you'd never have to waste time again looking for lost paperwork.[4] You'll need to block out a couple of hours in your diary for getting the system set up, of course. And that will be time well spent.

If you had a school run rota, you wouldn't have to take the kids to school or collect them on at least a couple of days a week. Think how much time that would save you. Of course, you'd have to spend a bit of time on the phone to other parents organising it, but it will be a worthwhile investment of time.

Train yourself never to think, "If only I'd done that ..." without questioning what you can do now to make sure it doesn't happen again. And use the strategies in this book to make sure you actually get around to doing it. Because, as you well know if you recognise yourself here, that's the challenge, and it comes down to how much you really want to save the time.

---

[4] I'm assuming here, perhaps rashly, that you're actually going to use the system once you have it.

DON'T DO
TOO MUCH

If your life is permanently overfull, it may be that you're just doing too much. If you're happy that way, then fine, but are you sure? (If you're reading this book it suggests that life is not exactly as you'd like it to be.)

And sometimes the answer is a drastic one. If an editor is asked to trim an article or a book down by a smidgeon, they'll cut out a few words here or half a line there. But if they need to cut it down by, say, 10 per cent, the only way to do it is to cut out whole sections. You can't lose that much material by trimming a word here and a phrase there. The only thing that will do the trick is major surgery.

The same goes for your life. If you can fit everything in, but it's sometimes a bit of a rush, this book will give you a few nifty time-saving techniques to do the job nicely. But if you're always rushed off your feet and stressed with it, you need to drop a part of your life. It sounds brutal, but it's the only way.

It may be that your commitments have just grown over time or as your life changes, and you've not dropped anything as a result (new job requiring longer hours at work, having children, etc.). In which case, maybe you need to have a good think about the whole picture and find something that can give, at least for a while.

I've known people in this situation step down from committees, change jobs to somewhere with a shorter commute, or even give up work altogether if they can afford to. If you're going to retain your sanity, something has to give. Might as well face it sooner rather than later and save yourself a lot of stress.

Even if you feel you're letting someone down, at least you know you're giving everyone else so much more of yourself. And at least the person *you* feel you've let down knows where he or she is and can reorganise, instead of being routinely let down because you ran out of time. In the long run you'll feel less guilty this way too.

DON'T WASTE
YOUR DOWN TIME

Are you sure you have too much to do? I'm not trying to be funny, but most of us get some free time. It's just that we don't spend it twiddling our thumbs. If you choose to go to the gym, play a sport, watch TV, read the paper, socialise, walk the dog, take an evening class or have a bath, these are all leisure activities. No one has to do these things.[5]

Many of us who think our days are too full are actually spending a fair bit of time doing things by choice. They may be things you are committed to doing, and you have to put them on your to-do list in order to fit them in, but they're still optional leisure activities. So perhaps your life isn't as busy as you think.

The thing is that as soon as we have time, we tend to fill it, as we've seen. And that's just fine. No point sitting around thumb-twiddling. Just be aware that you make choices constantly about how you're going to spend your time, and there's no point complaining afterwards. If you don't want your time to be spent with the kids or the dogs, don't have them. If you don't want to fit in time for the gym, stop going.

I'm not trying to be negative here and tell you to give things up. What I'm suggesting is that you remind yourself from time to time that you're doing this thing because you chose to do it. So enjoy it instead of feeling hassled and stressed – or of course give it up if you no longer want to choose it.[6]

[5] Yes, even walking the dog. You didn't have to get a pet, it's not compulsory. Although I wouldn't advise skipping too many baths.
[6] If you can. Obviously you're stuck with the kids and the dog, but you don't have to have any more.

BE RELIABLE

I have a mate who always used to be late for everything. That's if he turned up at all. He rarely returned calls, and the only thing you could count on him for was to miss important events. His unreliability was legendary. It irritated all his friends, but we all learned to live with it because we so enjoyed his company when he graced us with it.

I remember being stunned a few years ago when he actually turned up on time. I wasn't ready at all, and had planned lunch for 3 o'clock because he'd said he'd arrive at noon and I was making the usual allowance. I asked him what had happened and he told me he'd decided to stop being unreliable as he'd realised it just wasn't fair on other people. Simple as that. And do you know, I've never known him be significantly late since.

Now trust me, if he can do it so can you. If you're prone to let people down or turn up late, it's never too late to change. It's just a matter of realising, as he did, that being late and unreliable is simply unfair on other people. It's disrespectful, just like your mother always told you. Sure, we were all happy to forgive him, but that didn't mean it wasn't an inconvenience. And I'm sure some people found it harder to live with than I did.

Not only that, but he tells me his life is much simpler now he knows where to be when. He's more organised and he can meet all his commitments far more easily. So everyone wins.

Don't wait for people to change

I'm now going to directly contradict the last thing I said. So, with the exception of my friend from the previous page,[7] people don't change. If they're tricky, over-sensitive, slow, unreliable, bossy or anything else, they always will be.

Why am I telling you this? Well, because when you organise your life, you have to fit parts of it around other people. You can't exist in isolation, and you don't control the other people you're fitting around.

If you have a friend who always talks you into staying out for just one more drink, and then just one more, don't plan yourself an early night and a clear head in the morning. You need to build in allowance for the way people are, don't blithely expect them to behave the way you'd like them to. If your mother-in-law always brings the kids home late, or can be counted on to interfere when you're cooking Sunday lunch, then expect it to happen again. If it doesn't it will be a welcome surprise, but in fact it will happen again, you know it will.

Personally, I find that a lot of my stress comes from other people not behaving as I'd like them to (I don't care what that says about me, it's their fault). So I'm not good at this. But I do know that the way to a calmer life is not to wait for them to change, but to stop expecting it. If you can just build their idiosyncracies into your plans, life will be so much simpler.

---

[7] And you, of course, if you're planning to become more reliable.

Write lists

Whenever life gets really busy, it always helps to write lists. You can put all those things you're trying to remember down on one sheet, and that frees up your head space – to think about other things.

Mind you, a long list can look pretty daunting, and the thought of getting started on it can make your heart sink. I had an aunt who was a brilliant list maker, and who taught me how to make any list seem manageable. She said you should always start your list with three things:

- something really quick and easy
- something you'll enjoy
- something you've already done.

This means that you'll get off to a good start and rattle through the first few things. Once you've got those first three ticks at the top of the list, it will all start to look much more achievable.

GET OFF TO
A FLYING START

OK, now you've got at least three ticks at the top of your list. You're doing well. So what's next?

The next thing to do is the thing you're dreading. Maybe it's hard work, or perhaps it's difficult, or simply downright boring. Maybe you're inclined to put it off because you haven't quite worked out yet how to tackle it. Well, you can't avoid it for ever. But you can make sure it's not hanging over you any longer. Come on, I know it's a pain but let's just get it over with.

I know two friends who were moving house together. The day of the move they hired a van. One of them was all for getting the big heavy furniture loaded first and out of the way, and then sorting out the easy, lighter bits and pieces. The other wanted to do everything else first and leave the heavy stuff until last. But it still had to be done. The first approach at least meant the pair of them could spend the rest of the day with a feeling of satisfaction, rather than a feeling of dread. Because that's what it's all about.

Visualise the finished thing

I have a friend who tells me the only way she can face the ironing is to imagine herself next day opening her wardrobe and being able to choose anything she wants to wear, instead of being restricted to those few things that are still unworn and unrumpled.

I also know a chap who can only face the routine tidy and clearout of his sitting room by visualising how it will look when it's finished. Sometimes he even decides to try swapping around some of the furniture to make it more interesting.

So next time you're daunted by a task, think about how you'll feel and what you'll enjoy once it's complete. If it's enough to motivate someone to do the ironing, it's got to be a pretty powerful technique.

HAVE LESS

A great deal of time gets spent on things. Or stuff. Making space for them, tidying them away, setting them up, cleaning them, fixing them, replacing them, getting rid of them; whether it's books or gadgets or clothes or music or toys or stationery or cars or anything else.

When you buy a new DVD player, for example, how much time will that take? You have to spend time selecting it, then you have to buy it, maybe physically go and fetch it. Then you have to move the old one out of the way, and decide what to do with it, and then do it. Next you have to set up the new one – plug it in and so on. Now you need to go through the set-up procedure,[8] complete with frustration and swearing and cursing. How long did all that take? And if it doesn't run smoothly you'll have to think about repairs in due course as well. Are you sure, with your busy life, that it's really worth it? What else could you have achieved in that time?

If you didn't have these things, you wouldn't be spending all that time on them. Stands to reason, doesn't it? I'm not really suggesting you convert to the life of an ascetic minimalist, unless that grabs you. But I am saying that every time you acquire something new you should be aware of the time you'll need to invest in it. And, if your time is short, perhaps it might be wise to cut back on some of that stuff.

---

[8] Unless, like me, you can delegate it to an 11-year-old who is already way ahead of you.

Have a
packing list

One of the most useful and time-saving lists you can have is for when you go away. Packing is so much simpler if you're just working through a list without having to think much. So keep a permanent packing list on your PC and print it off every time you go away. This way you can update it easily as things change. And you can remove things this time round if you don't want them for this trip (no point packing your passport if you're not going abroad, or your sun cream in the middle of winter).

This is especially invaluable if you have children, and not only because you're packing for more people. As they get older you can delete items from the permanent list, such as nappies, buggy, dummy, armbands, blanky (or whatever your child's comforter is called).

You don't have to stick to items to go in the suitcase. You can also include on your list other things you need to do (water the plants, stop the milk delivery), and other things you need to pack (items for the car, food to take if you're self-catering). Whatever works for you, in other words. There, now your holiday will get off to a much more relaxed start, and you won't find you've left something vital behind.

GET INTO
GOOD
HABITS

Are you forgetful? Of course you are – at least some of the time. We all are. The people who look as if they have perfect memories actually just have good systems for coping with memory lapses. And that's all you need too.

One of the simplest techniques is to have a habit that is so ingrained that you don't need to remember it. One of my children has a pretty poor short-term memory and when he started at secondary school one of his worries was that he'd forget where he'd left his jacket. As he had to rush for a bus in the morning he couldn't afford to waste precious minutes searching the house for it. So he trained himself that every time he came home at the end of the day, the first thing he'd do was to take off his jacket and hang it up inside the door. We all helped him remember for the first few days, and within a week it was automatic. You see, the point was that he didn't have to remember it – he didn't have to think about it at all. And he's never yet lost it or left it anywhere else.

This doesn't work for occasional things, but it works for things you have to remember regularly. Before you take the recipe book off the shelf, you turn on the oven. Before you leave your office you switch on your voicemail. Before you go upstairs to bed you lock the front door. Not at any time during the evening, but just before you put your foot on the bottom stair so it will feel odd climbing the stairs if you haven't just done it. It will take a few days for the habit to settle, and after that you'll never have to think about it again. Bliss!

HAVE A PLACE
FOR IT

Where do your car keys live when you're at home? I don't mean where *should* they live, but where do they actually live? Surprisingly few people have a single answer to this question – usually they'll tell you, "Well, they're supposed to be in the kitchen drawer/in my pocket/on the hall table/hanging on the hook, but I can never find them there when I need them."

If you're one of those people, you may be surprised and reassured[9] to know that there are people in the world who have never, ever lost their car keys. Or their mobile phone. Or their wallet. Or their pen. Or their glasses. And the reason for this is because these things really truly do always live in the same place. Every time they open the kitchen drawer, there are the keys.

This is an extension of the previous point. Instead of doing something at a certain time, you make a habit of keeping it in a certain place. Again, it takes a few days to establish, but once you've made that effort, you'll find it feels so odd to put your keys/mobile/ wallet down anywhere else that you just can't do it. You have to put them where they belong. In fact, make it a habit never to let go of the keys, the phone or whatever it is until it's in its place. That way it will feel so odd to drop your keys on the table, for instance, that you'll notice if you do it and stop yourself.

There you are – one more thing off your mind, and no more wasted time spent searching the house for your keys.

[9] Or irritated ...

FILE YOUR WEEK

I f you're not naturally organised, this is going to sound scarily hyper-efficient. But, believe me, it will make your life so much easier.

What you do is find yourself a file – a decent-sized one – and put everything you need for the week in it. You can be really organised and sort it out on a Sunday evening, or you can do it on Monday morning if that level of efficiency is taking things too far for you.

So what do you put in it? Well, it might contain the agenda for that vital meeting on Wednesday, plus the belated birthday card to give your brother when you see him,[10] the train tickets for your journey on Friday, your MoT and car insurance paperwork so you can tax the car, that letter from school with all the details for end-of-term activities this week, the book you need to return to your boss ... and so on. You can add things, of course, as the week goes on, but don't add next week's stuff until Sunday or it will become so cumbersome you'll stop using it, which will defeat the object.

If you don't go out to work, the file might in fact be a drawer in the hall table, or it might be a bag that lives in the car so it's always with you (if you get about by car). It doesn't have to be a literal file, although this may well be the best option if you commute to work.

Hyper-efficient it may be, but there's nothing wrong with that. And I'd hope that you're already starting to see how much easier it will make your life – and you haven't even tried it yet.

---

[10] Although once you follow all the tips in this book belated cards should become a thing of the past.

KEEP A
NOTEBOOK

Those last couple of points were really useful (I hope you'll agree) for many things, but they don't help you remember one-off things. Like reminding you to check the cinema listings for the weekend, or print off extra copies of those minutes, or invite Matthew and Sarah over for dinner, or buy your child a protractor, or let your PA know you'll be in late on Monday.

The solution here is to keep a notebook and pen about your person at all times.[11] You can get one small enough to fit in your pocket. Just jot down everything you need to remember. It clears your mind wonderfully – of course once it's down on paper you no longer have to retain it inside your head – which makes for much less stress.

Again, it will take a few days to get in the habit, but once you have done your life will be so much simpler you'll wonder why you didn't start doing it years ago.

[11] Use the advice on the previous page to make sure you don't lose it.

Count your bags

Have you ever got home from a shopping trip to find you've left one of your bags somewhere (I presume you have no idea where; that's usually the way)? Or been on holiday to discover that one piece of luggage doesn't seem to have made it home with you? It's easily done, and hugely frustrating at the very least.

The answer is simple. Make sure you always know how many items you have with you, and count them in and out every time you stop and start moving. Please don't ask me whether your shoulder bag counts as an item of luggage, or whether that includes your hat. I really don't care – include your children in the total if you want to (and if they're with you). It's only you who needs to know what's included. It's important that you know whether your shoulder bag counts towards the total or not, but either way is fine.

Now every time you put your bags down – in a café, at a shop counter, by baggage reclaim, on the bus – do a quick count-up. Same again when you pick them up to move on.

By the way, the one thing that bugs me about this system, despite the fact that it really does work, is that every so often you'll find yourself thinking, "If I just put these two bags inside this big one, it will be easier to carry." It certainly will, but you need to remember to re-educate your internal counting mechanism to allow for the fact that you're now carrying, say, three items instead of five.

STREAMLINE YOUR
WORKLOAD

If you want to get through your workload faster, it makes sense to put your tasks into related groups. It's up to you what these are, so long as they're logical. For example, you might get all your kitchen chores done first and then all the upstairs ones. Or you might deal with your emails and then your phone calls, and then do the research for your presentation.

It's always quicker to do things that belong in the same category at the same time – you'll be in the same place with the same resources to hand. And it's also more efficient because your mind doesn't have to make so many leaps. If you have to keep switching function between, say, concentrated reading or writing, and then talking to other people, it will take you a while to get up to speed each time. Far better to focus your brain on one group of tasks until they're all done, and then switch to the next.

Streamline your movements

When you're really busy, you can fit more jobs into a short time if you make every move count. This might sound like an unnecessary effort, and indeed it is if you have all the time in the world, but it's a very effective – and satisfying – thing to do when time is short.

For example, why go upstairs empty-handed? There's almost always clean laundry to put away, new soap to take up to the bathroom, or kids' toys to return to the bedroom. And there's often stuff to bring back downstairs too – dirty laundry, rubbish from the bins, your current reading book to take on the train to work. Get into the habit of checking for anything to take with you, and you'll save yourself countless journeys over time.

My morning school run routine with the children is timed to the minute (so I don't have to get up any earlier than I must). I grab the hairbrush on my way to the kitchen from unbolting the front door, I get the cereal out of the cupboard as I'm passing to let the dog out in the garden. And so on. When things go smoothly it's probably not essential but the efficient feel of it keeps me amused. And when something interrupts the routine, my streamlined system can make all the difference.

Multitask

One of my favourite multitasking stories comes from my brother-in-law. He was hopelessly map reading in the car, and going on and on about where he thought they ought to be but didn't seem to be. In the end his wife, who was driving, said, "Do you know, for a bloke you're very good at multitasking. You're managing to be boring *and* irritating at the same time."

Well, boring and irritating, both at once, won't get much done. But making a phone call while you're cooking the dinner – now that's another story. If you've got a long list of things to do, it makes sense to do more than one at a time.

Obviously some jobs won't thank you for doubling them up. It will take twice as long to get that report written if you're doing it in the slack periods during parents' evening. But some tasks lend themselves very well to it – especially those which are relatively mindless, or at least one of the two is.

You can work through your mail while you're on hold for some organisation that takes forever to answer its phones. You can get some general reading done during ad breaks on TV. You can plan your meals for the week while you're driving to the shops. A bit of judicious multitasking will save you plenty of time.

BUILD UP A
STOCKPILE

If, like me, you have children, you'll doubtless hate that moment of realising that if your child is going to a party on Saturday, that means you have to find time between now and then to go out and buy a present for the child whose party it is. And a card. And wrapping paper.

Unless you're my wife, who hoards such things. I like to tease her about it but secretly I have to admit[12] how sensible it is. Sometimes, if she knows the child well, she'll go out and choose something specific for them if there's time, but she also keeps several presents in a cupboard ready to wrap (in paper she also has at the ready). Needless to say she also keeps a plentiful supply of birthday cards to suit all occasions. And I must confess it saves a lot of time and a great deal of stress.

You can, of course, do the same thing with adult presents and cards. Not to mention stockpiling other things you know you'll need sooner or later, such as light bulbs or batteries or stamps.

[12] No, of course not to her.

DOUBLE
UP

You know when you go away overnight or for the weekend? One of the things you have to do is to put together an overnight bag of toothbrush, toothpaste, moisturiser, razor or whatever it is you need for your ablutions.

Well, here's a thought. Wouldn't it be great to save the time and hassle of doing this? Of course it would – and you can. Just have a ready-packed travel spongebag permanently at the ready. Two of everything – one for home, one for travel. Now isn't that easier?

While you're thinking in this kind of efficient mode, there are other things you can double up too. Anything, in fact, that you find yourself needing in two different places. Scissors in the kitchen *and* the living room. Sellotape in the home office *and* the kids' bedrooms. Hand cream in the bathroom *and* the kitchen. Look, only you know what you're always running up and down stairs for but, whatever it is, double it up.

Turn your toothbrush upside down

When I was young I was always told that if I wanted to remember something I should put a knot in my handkerchief. Well, trouble is that no one really carries a handkerchief any more (except maybe great aunts). I've tried knotting tissues but they just tear. However, there are other ways to remember things.

If I think of something at bedtime that I mustn't forget in the morning, I turn my toothbrush upside down. This might sound daft, but I know I'll use my toothbrush in the morning, and I'll look at it and think, "What on earth is that doing upside down?" Then I'll remember. And, yes, I always do remember.[13] The trick is that as you turn it over you have to visualise yourself doing whatever it is – taking the cat to the vet, or putting the CD in your briefcase, or taking the meringues out of the oven. That way, you'll know in the morning what you were supposed to remember.

Of course there are other ways of using this trick. You can hang your bag or jacket on a different hook to remind you when you leave that your mobile isn't in it because it's on charge. Or put an upside-down pudding basin in the middle of the kitchen table to signify that the plants need watering. In fact, you can be as quirky as you like, because the important thing is that when you next look at the thing, you need to think, "What on earth ...?"

[13] Of course I may have forgotten again before I actually get to do whatever it is, but that's another matter.

PIN A NOTE
ON THE DOOR

I know it's obvious, but do you always do it? If you're forgetful when you're in a rush, why not just leave a note on the door where you'll see it as you go out: 'Buy eggs' or whatever.

Of course you don't have to pin it to the door. Just put it wherever you're most likely to see it. In your sock drawer, next to your car keys, or in the fruit bowl. If you're leaving a note for your teenager, try taping it to the TV screen. If it's for your daughter maybe you should stick it on the mirror. If you feed the dog every morning, put it by the dog food. Or it can go in the car. Or put it in the fridge.[14]

I can never remember which child takes what games kit/recorder/spellings/swimming kit, etc. into school on which days. So there's a note permanently pinned up in the hall telling me. It makes life so much easier in the mornings.

All you need to do now is remember where you keep the Blu-Tack...

[14] Works for me every time.

BE DECISIVE
ABOUT MESS

You know all that clutter and mess lying around your house or office? Do you know why it's there? You might think it's because you haven't got room for it, or because you haven't got time to clear it away. But you'd be wrong.

It's very rare for clutter to build up because there isn't time to sort it out. I know this because I know some people with almost no time who have no clutter either, so it can't be that. I've found out what it is though, and I can tell you. It's being indecisive that creates clutter. Bringing things into the room or house or office without thinking through whether you actually have a use for them. Not being sure where to put things away. Thinking you need something despite all the evidence (i.e. you never use it), so not being sure it's OK to get rid of it.

If you were clear about what you were doing, when you'd finished with things, what they were for, where they lived and so on, there'd be no clutter. That's how all those 'busy but tidy' people do it.

I know you can't turn into someone who is decisive about these things overnight. But if you understand what's causing the problem you can at least start to address it, instead of blaming it all on lack of time.

LEARN HOW TO TIDY

Tidying is a miserable, thankless task. At least it always seems like it, although actually it's quite satisfying once it's done. Even if it is a bit like banging your head against a brick wall (it's great when it stops). Actually, tidying is much easier when you know what you're doing. It's a skill like any other, but few of us have ever been taught how to do it. Our parents yelled at us as kids to "Tidy your room!" but they never told us how. Well, my mother never told me anyway.

Once you know what you're doing, it's much less daunting. Whether it's routine tidying in the house or clearing out the attic before moving house. Here's how it goes:

- Have a rubbish bag with you.
- Tidy up related objects first. Pick up all the books, or all the rubbish, or all the work-related stuff, or all the clothes, or all the cuddly toys.
- Tidy up specific parts of the room next. Clear the floor, or the table, or the top of the fridge. Work your way through these one at a time.
- Make a pile of everything that you don't know what to do with. These things are often the biggest problem when you're tidying – you keep picking them up and putting them down again because you're not sure where they go. When everything else is done, tackle this pile and decide where you're going to keep lengths of string, or interesting newspaper clippings, or the guarantee for your new laptop.
- Make piles of anything that doesn't live in this room. One pile to go to the kitchen, another for upstairs and so on. Put these away last (or you'll get distracted and never come back).

The next time you look up, the room will be almost done, and you'll wonder what the fuss was.

Get the kids working

If you have kids, you really understand the challenges of having a long to-do list. There's a never-ending round of tidying up, laundry, cooking (can't just grab a snack because you haven't the energy to cook), school runs, uniform labelling, music practice and all the rest.

So get your kids to muck in as much as possible. It's unlikely that you could (or should) get your kids doing so much that life's easier than it was before they came along, but they can certainly do their bit. From an early age you can teach children some basic chores. This will show them that helping round the house is normal, and means they will at least do some of the work that their presence generates.

If you can't think of any suitable tasks to offload, here are some ideas of tasks that kids as young as five can do – in some cases even younger:

- lay the table
- load the dishwasher
- wash up
- hang up bath towels (just don't expect them to be too tidy)
- put clothes in the laundry
- load the washing machine and turn it on
- load the tumble dryer and turn it on
- put clean clothes away in the wardrobe
- unpack the shopping and put it away.

There, that should get you started. By the time they're teenagers they should take chores for granted, and your life should be at least that little bit easier.

DON'T DO IT YOURSELF

Following on from the last point,[15] once you've delegated a chore to someone else, don't under any circumstances do it yourself. This applies at home and at work, and anywhere else such as committees or local clubs.

Once someone discovers that if they don't do their own tasks, you'll do them instead; why would they ever bother to do them? So you have to be firm and stick to your guns. If that means your children end up with nothing clean to wear at the weekend because they haven't put their dirty clothes in the laundry, well that might teach them something. Ditto if the family can't eat off the table because it's still covered in shopping. Or your PA can't find the website they want because they didn't make a note of it when you asked them to.

If you relent, you're stuffed. And the longer it takes before you relent, the longer they'll hang on next time, waiting for you to step in. So you have to say no and mean it, however stinky your child's bedroom gets, or however many meals you can't cook because the food all went off waiting for someone to unpack it.

If you've already fallen into this trap, then tell everyone that you won't be doing their jobs any more and *stick to it*. They may not believe you at first, but they pretty soon will when the thing just doesn't get done.

[15] Well, go and read it now if you haven't already, and stop being so unorganised. It will take you longer to get through the book, you know.

Give false
deadlines

Some people are always late. Whether you're meeting up for a drink, or relying on their report so you can complete your work, it can be an infuriating waste of time. How are you ever supposed to get anything done when people around you are letting you down?

There's a simple answer though. Just agree to meet at 7.45pm if you're planning to be there at 8pm. Or tell them you need their report for Friday when actually you won't need it before the following Wednesday. You know how late each person is likely to run, so adjust the deadline accordingly.

There is one thing you have to be careful about – never let them know you're doing this. If they once start to suspect, they'll mentally adjust the deadline back again, and then overrun it. It's a shame, because it's very tempting when they apologise yet again for being late to say, "That's OK. I didn't get here until 8pm myself. I only said 7.45 because I knew you'd be late." Tempting, but fatal. This is one secret you have to keep to yourself.

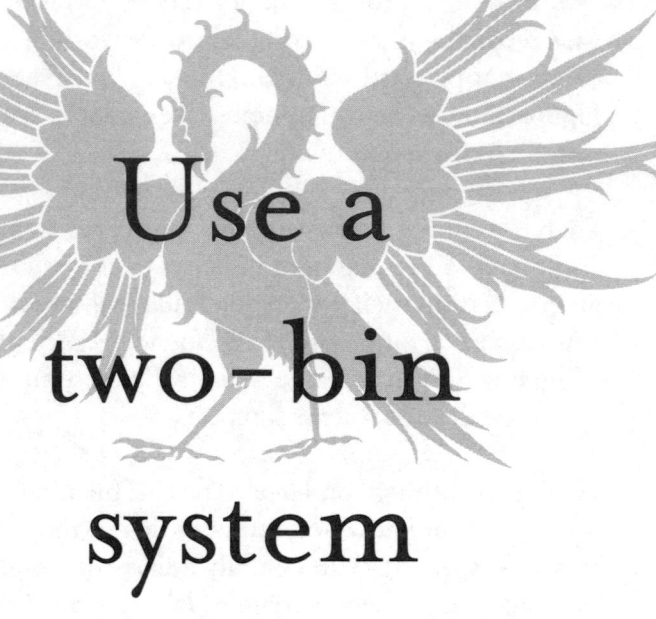

Use a two-bin system

How often do you get caught out looking in the cupboard and finding there are no more baked beans, or discovering when you go to bed that you've run out of toothpaste? You need a two-bin system.

The two-bin system is a method of stock control that's been superseded in business. It ties up too much working capital and is now regarded as being lumbering and out of date. But, on a personal level, it's just what you need. You're not likely to be investing thousands in raw materials, you're just buying the odd tin of beans or tube of toothpaste and the cash flow is barely an issue.

So here's how it works. You have two of everything. One that's on the go and one spare; the toothpaste you're using now and the spare tube in the bathroom cupboard. As soon as you finish one you have a spare, and you immediately buy a new spare. If you don't buy it now – and you may not need me to tell you this – you'll forget about it until you've run out.

Have a rule in your household (and getting kids to cooperate with this will be your biggest challenge, I can tell you) that whenever anyone starts the last packet, tube, box, tin, bottle or bag of anything, they immediately write it down on the shopping list so that a spare can be bought in plenty of time.

HAVE A
SHOPPING LIST

Even if you live alone, have a pad and pen, that never move, on which you write down anything you need to buy. Next time you go shopping the list is largely written for you and you won't keep running out of things. If there's more than one of you in the house this is even more essential.

If you already do this, you may find it hard to believe but there really are people who don't, and have to make up a shopping list from scratch every time they go out.

If you *don't* already do this, look, you see, some people can't even believe that you're seriously trying to get things done without a permanent shopping list pad.

Read faster

I'm no speed-reader, although I can read pretty fast. I taught myself to do this when I realised just how much time it would save me with all the paperwork I was expected to get through at work.

It's well worth buying a book on speed-reading[16] or finding some good software. Broadly speaking, though, the gist is that slow readers read every word, moving their eyes along a line until they get to the end, and then moving back to the left-hand end of the next line. Fast readers, on the other hand, barely move their eyes at all, but run them down the middle of the page taking in the edges of lines peripherally. They scan, looking for the relevant information.

You can certainly practise doing this yourself, and skipping unnecessary chunks of text if the writer is getting a bit wordy or off the point. If you have a lot of material to get through, even a slight increase in speed could free up a decent chunk of time.

[16] You should be able to read it quite fast.

KEEP TIME

Recognise this scenario? You're just getting the dinner on before going to collect one of the kids, when you realise you've lost track of time and should have left five minutes ago. Or you're just working on something on the computer when you realise your next meeting is already starting and you haven't got your paperwork ready yet.

We all do this, and the answer is to set a timer to go off when you need to stop what you're doing (NB this may be a few minutes before you have to start doing the next thing). You may have a watch or mobile phone with a timer – or could get one – or you might prefer to use a kitchen timer. OK, you may feel a bit of a prat walking around the office with a kitchen timer round your neck, but it will do the trick. And wearing it around your neck means you can't go out of earshot.

GET AHEAD
OF YOURSELF

Suppose, taking an example from the previous point, you have a few minutes to spare to work on your proposal before your meeting starts. Maybe you've taken the suggestion about setting a timer to go off five minutes before you have to leave your desk. Even so, wouldn't it be great if, when it's time to go, you can just grab your paperwork and leave the office because you've already sorted it out?

This kind of strategy can save you so much panic and stress. Suppose, when you rush for that train, you know the ticket is in your wallet because you put it there yesterday? Or you know your theatre or cinema tickets are in the car because that's where you put them last time you drove somewhere.

These things make for a much calmer life. If you know your child has to take something to school on Monday, put it in the car or in their bag now. Put the passports out two days before you go on holiday so you can stop fretting about forgetting them. Once you learn to get ahead of yourself it gets easier and easier. At the first sign of worry about what might happen, just do it now and there'll be no panic later.

REMEMBER
BIRTHDAYS

Some people just do remember birthdays and some just don't. Correction. Some people have a system to remind them of birthdays and some just don't. If you'd like to be the kind of person who remembers, all you need is a system like other people have.

There are lots of ways of doing it, all of which are variations on the same theme.[17] You need a diary that has birthdays written in it. It's not that complicated really. If you use software such as Outlook that's ideal, as you put the information in once and it pings at you for evermore. But a birthday book or yearly diary will do as well.

If you use a yearly diary you'll need to copy all the birthdays over to your new diary each year. It really won't take long unless you have vast numbers of friends and family whose birthdays you celebrate. Preferably, copy these dates across as soon as you get the new diary. Failing that, the best approach is to keep the old diary somewhere really irritating, such as on your computer keyboard, until you've got around to it. If you put it tidily on a shelf I think we all know what's going to happen ...

---

[17] Apart from my favourite one – wait for your wife to remind you. But apparently that doesn't count.

GET
CHRISTMAS
WRAPPED UP

If you're one of those people who always leaves Christmas shopping and preparations to the last minute, and then gets stressed by the whole exercise, there is an answer.

The usual approach to this is to promise yourself you'll get ahead and then, of course, it doesn't happen. Once December gets into its stride you're already running late and can't find the time.

The answer is to have Christmas all but sorted by the end of November. Look through those mail order catalogues that start hitting your doormat in September (if not earlier) and actually place an order instead of putting it on your list of things to do later.

If Christmas cooking is part of the stress, either buy in ready-made food or do everything you can ahead of time and put it in the freezer by the beginning of December. You can freeze stuffings, sauces, all the trimmings. Then you only have to cook the equivalent of a Sunday roast on the day.

And if you find Christmas really stressful, start buying presents for next time in January – before you've forgotten the strain you're trying to avoid. They'll be cheap in the sales then too.

Treat yourself

When you have a major task to get through, it can be so daunting you don't know where to start. Whether it's organising Christmas, or doing a major piece of research at work, or packing up to move house.

You know the expression, "How would you eat an elephant? One bite at a time." So follow the principle of breaking it down into small tasks.[18] Then allow yourself a treat at the end of each chunk of elephant. Maybe a cup of tea, or five minutes browsing on the Internet, or an unrelated task you enjoy and can slot into the gap, such as walking the dog. It's best to avoid biscuits or chocolate (and if you can't, look out for the companion book to this one: *How to Lose Weight Without Being Miserable*).

If the task is a long one, perhaps you need to give yourself a bigger reward every few chunks. So long as you spend most of your time getting on with the job rather than rewarding yourself, it can be a good way to get through. And, as always, it won't be long before you suddenly realise you're over halfway and can see the light at the end of the tunnel.

[18] Or should that be tusks?

FIND A SIXPENCE

Here's another way to make certain tasks more approachable, to encourage you to get on with them. I have a friend who works in PR. She tells me that if she has a load of journalists to call, who might be stroppy or just not there, she makes sure that about every tenth call she makes is to someone she knows will be friendly. That way, just as she's starting to feel demoralised, she'll get a boost.

This is a clever ploy which I've copied myself. There are lots of tasks that are hard work but have their high spots, and if you can spread those highlights out across the task it will keep you going. Often it's people who lift your day, and making certain phone calls can often be the thing we need to give us a lift.

Be decisive

I know a chap who just can't make decisions. Every time you ask him if he'd like tea or coffee he dithers for 10 minutes. He used to do a job he hated and it took him 7 years to make the decision to leave and get another job. Once he had a family his house quickly became too small and he said he'd need to move. By the time he did, his oldest child was six.

This is 'not getting things done' on a grand scale. But it illustrates a clear point – you'll never get anything done until you know what it is you want to do. So if you're not naturally a decisive person, you need to learn a few decision-making skills so that at least you know what's on your to-do list.

You'll find some general techniques on the next few pages, but the root of the solution is to recognise that you could achieve more if you didn't put off decisions. Then all you need to do is start with the decision to become more decisive.

Lay the groundwork first

It's easy to delay a decision because you don't have enough information to hand. Of course you can't make decisions without the facts. Well, I say that, yet I'm notorious for making decisions without the facts, and lack of decisiveness has never been a problem for me. Some would say I was too decisive ... but if you're prone to indecision I suspect that you're the type of person who likes to have all the facts to hand first.

There's a certain inertia that sets in when you put off deciding what to do without really noticing you've put it off. And then nothing happens for ages. The reason is generally that deep down you're aware you don't have all the information you need, but you're not consciously addressing this and setting about assembling the information you need. When other decisions and actions depend on the decision you're delaying, that's when you feel you're not getting anything done. You aren't.

So you need to recognise what's going on and actively go and collect the information you need. Opinions, statistics, prices, whatever it is that's required. If you still can't decide, question what more you need to feed into the equation and then go and get it. Once you have all the facts and figures it should be easy to make the decision.

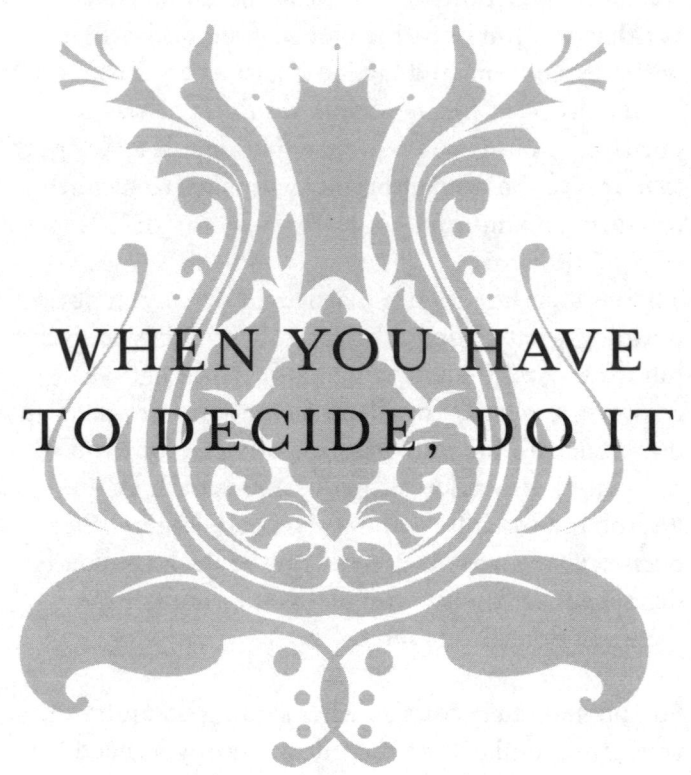

WHEN YOU HAVE
TO DECIDE, DO IT

If you keep putting off a decision, you don't solve anything, you just make things worse. So for every decision you need to make, identify the time by when it needs to be made. Then make sure you have all the information you need and make the decision by then.

For big decisions this may be some time ahead. Where are you going on holiday this year? You need to know how much holiday entitlement you have, what you can afford, when will be the best time to be away (no point booking somewhere that's in the middle of monsoon season), what the children's school holiday dates are, when your partner will be free, where the rest of the family fancy going, and so on. You'll need time to assemble all that information.

On the other hand, if you leave it too late it could cost more or even be fully booked. So set yourself a deadline and commit to making a decision by, say, the end of April. Then when the time comes, do it.

For smaller decisions, the time to do it is often now. If you're tidying the house and you're not sure where to keep this collection of letters you keep meaning to reply to, just make a decision. Otherwise you'll waste time thinking about it now, and then have to think about it again later. The answer's not going to get any clearer, so just save yourself time by getting the decision over with.

TOSS A
COIN

So you've weighed up all the information you collected and you still can't decide. Tea or coffee? Hand in your notice or stick with the job for another 6 months?

If you have all the information you can get and it doesn't point you firmly in either direction, just toss a coin. Yes, I'm serious. What else can you do? I know it's easy for me to say – I have a bit of a habit of tossing the coin first without ever collecting the facts – but there comes a point when you have to recognise (important bit coming up …) that *making a decision is more important than what the decision is.* Yep, you'll never get anything done if you don't get on and decide. The kettle will have gone cold, or you'll end up spending another 6 months in the job waiting to make the decision, even if that wasn't the best choice.

If one option were distinctly better than the others, you'd have established that by now. You have all the information. If you can't see a clear favourite at this point, it's down to chance or whim or gut instinct anyway, so just toss a coin.

If you can't decide whether to change jobs, how can you decide whether to move house? Where you can afford to go on holiday this year? Or when? Should you trade in your car or might you get a company car? Should you enrol on that training course? You see, all those other things won't get done either if you don't get on and make your decision.

Tell everyone what you've decided

Once you've made your decision, there's no point keeping it to yourself. Not that you need to go round boring everyone with the information that you've finally decided to have a cup of tea. But any decision that affects other people needs to be passed on.

I would hope that this is standard practice at work. Nevertheless, it's easy to miss out the odd person who needs to know. Not only does this risk offending them, it also means they can't do their job as efficiently as they should. So you need to be sure that you've told everyone who needs to know.

At home, the same applies. No good deciding you'll go and see your mother on Friday if you don't tell her. And you need to be sure you tell everyone about the holiday rather than just booking it, otherwise your partner may say, "Aaargh! I didn't realise you were actually about to book it without saying so. I'm not free that week any more, my best friend's just fixed her wedding then." So come the end of April (or whenever) you need to tell the family, "Right, it's decided. We're going to go to Italy the first week in September. I'm about to book it."

Besides, people are always happier and more cooperative when they feel included. If you don't tell people what you've decided, not only can it cause practical problems later, it can also cause bad feeling.

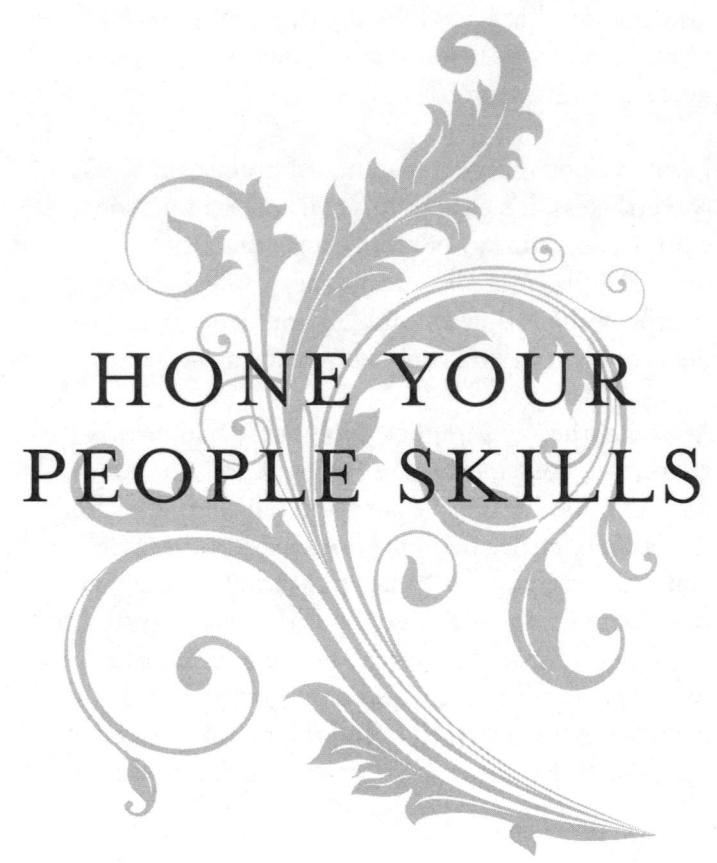

HONE YOUR
PEOPLE SKILLS

Some of us are naturally better than others at handling people. The key point I want to make here is that we can all improve, and that dealing with people better means you will get more done.[19]

Why will you get more done? For lots of reasons, including:

- You're more likely to get others to cooperate and take some of your workload off you.
- You'll be better equipped to stop people dumping more work on you.
- You'll be less stressed if your personal and working relationships are smoother.
- If you can say clearly what you mean, people will be more able to do as you want.

So whatever your people skills are like, recognise that you can work on them and improve them in order to make your own life easier.

[19] OK, that was two points.

BE ASSERTIVE

Assertiveness is all about expressing facts and feelings clearly without emotions getting in the way. Submissive people find it hard to say how they feel or what they want. Dominant people use emotional levers such as anger or emotional blackmail. You'll get what you want best by being assertive – you won't rile anyone, you'll say what you mean clearly, and people will be happy to cooperate with you.

Of course this is all easier said than done. If you've never said boo to a goose it's going to be pretty hard asking your boss to enable you to leave work on time every day. But this is a skill you'll need if you're going to clear all those bits of time that get eaten up by other people's demands.

Once you've determined to be more assertive, you need to practise. In front of a mirror, in the car, and then in due course on other people. If you still find it hard, start with some easy conversations, or with people you'll never see again such as shop assistants or telephone helpdesks. (I don't mean phone them up specially – I just mean when something crops up.)

You need to be able to say what you want clearly and politely: "I find it very hard to manage if I don't get away from work on time. Please can we talk about strategies for making sure I can leave promptly at 5.30?" That's entirely reasonable and pleasant, and opens up the conversation clearly so you both know what you want to achieve.

LEARN TO
SAY NO

If you're someone who finds it hard to say no, it's no wonder you're reading this book. It's much harder to keep the workload down when you're taking on extra just because you can't find the words to say you don't want to do it.

So here are a few pointers to help you find the assertiveness to say no. You'll find the more you manage to say it, the easier it gets:

- It can seem brusque to say no flatly, so give an explanation. You've no obligation to do this, but you might feel happier. So you could say, "I can't do it, I'm afraid, I have to take my mother to the hospital on Thursday."
- Offer an alternative if you feel better for it, but make sure it's one you're genuinely happy to do: "I can't work on the report with you, but I'll read through it and comment, if you like."
- Suggest an alternative solution if you can. "I can't do that, but Jo might be able to" (only do this if Jo is assertive enough to say no if she wants to). Or maybe, "I haven't got time to go to the shops, but you can always buy it online. I can give you the website address."

All of these are ways of saying no that still sound helpful rather than obstructive. The more you practise them, the easier they get. Honest.

Stand your ground

Here's another technique that is quite challenging if assertiveness isn't your natural style, but will train your friends and colleagues that you're not a pushover. It's perfectly polite though, and entirely reasonable.

If someone is pushing you to do something you don't want to, you simply repeat your position like a stuck record (or a stuck CD if you're under about 30).[20] Suppose another parent asks you to pick up her child from school. It's a major pain because you're not going straight home that day to drop the child back. Just say, "I'd be happy to another day but I can't do Monday." If she persists you just repeat it: "I can't do Monday, we're going to Brownies after school." If she asks again, you say, "I really can't do Monday."

Now, you may be thinking I lied when I said this wouldn't sound rude. But I promise it won't because it's the other person who is deciding how many times to repeat this exchange. If she doesn't think it's rude to ask the same question for the third time, how can it be rude for you to make the same reply? If she doesn't like it, all she has to do is accept your answer and drop the subject.

[20] Although I'm not sure CDs repeat themselves like records do.

UNDERSTAND THICK SKINS

The last example I gave is also a good example of this principle. The thing to understand is that people who need telling something several times have thick enough skins to take it. If someone asks you something repeatedly, even though you keep saying no, they don't mind being told no repeatedly.

I used to have an employee who was always nattering. She never took any hints to stop, so when I walked past I'd say, "Come on, get on with your work!" in a jovial, half-joking, half-serious manner. It did the trick. I had a colleague who told me he'd feel far too embarrassed to say such a thing so bluntly. He'd feel he was being rude and imperious.

My colleague was judging himself out of context. It would indeed be rude and imperious to speak like that to many employees, and I wouldn't do it either. But this employee didn't respond to anything less. If she didn't want to be spoken to so firmly she'd have learned not to get caught nattering, or at least to get back to work in response to a raised eyebrow or a hint about how the morning was flying by.

Anyone who needs telling firmly, or telling several times, will think that's normal, trust me. Everyone else in their lives will be obliged to treat them the same way and they'll be quite used to it.

Say what
you mean

Some of us find this tricky and others don't. The problem arises especially when you're under-assertive and are trying to find a gentle way of saying something that, in truth, you could just say straight.

Suppose an elderly neighbour offers to sit with your toddler while you go to the shops. You don't actually want her to do this as you're not sure she could cope in an emergency. What you want to say is, "That's very kind but no thanks. I can manage fine. I'll take him with me." However, you're worried this will sound rude and abrupt after she's made such a kind offer, so you say, "Well, that's very kind ... I mean, I'm sure I'll be fine ... I wouldn't want to put you to any trouble, and I don't mind taking him with me, really." You may think you've said no, but your neighbour has heard a very rambling, "Yes, thank you." Later that day your neighbour arrives to babysit and you don't know what to do. Except, knowing you, you'll think the only polite thing is to leave your toddler in the hands of someone you're not sure is up to looking after him.

And if we rewind back to the start of that example, there's nothing wrong with saying, "That's very kind but no thanks. I can manage fine. I'll take him with me." And look at the trouble it would have saved.

Learn to say what you mean clearly with no unnecessary words, and when you get advance warning, practise what you're going to say to be sure it says what you mean it to.

Keep calm

Think about how you feel if someone tries getting you to do what they want by shouting or bursting into tears. It's not likely to help, is it? People don't respond well to emotional barrages of any kind. If you want people on side it really helps to express how you feel without negative emotion getting in the way.

I know one woman who manages to hyperventilate whever her children don't do what she wants (these are grown-up children by the way – I've not tried this technique on little ones but I doubt it would work). It works in the short term, but they avoid calling and visiting because they know what will happen. It's really not productive in the long run.

As soon as someone feels they are being attacked, verbally or emotionally or both, they become defensive. And you don't want to be dealing with defensive people – they're far less likely to help you get things done effectively.

COUNT TO TEN

If someone is really getting to you and there's a danger that you're going to lose your cool, don't let it happen. It will take twice as long to sort things out and may well leave bad feeling. Not to mention that it makes you look like someone who can't control their temper.

The best option here is to say something along the lines of, "I don't feel happy about this. Let's discuss it later," and then leave. You need to get out of the room before you blow. Once you've had time to calm down and think, you should be able to finish the conversation.

If you really can't leave, the best thing to do is to take a deep breath and count to ten. With luck that will calm you down enough to trust yourself to speak calmly. If you really can't say anything without getting emotional, just stay silent until you can.

See their

point of view

When you're really angry with someone, it's hard to hold a rational conversation with them. As I said before, it's best to avoid a conversation at all until you've calmed down. But how are you going to restart the conversation without getting angry again?

One of the best techniques is to work out what their perspective is. If you can put yourself in their shoes you may not agree with them, but at least you'll get an insight that should help you to stay calm and may help find a resolution. Which in turn will make you more productive and less stressed.

There are precious few people who will pick a fight with you for absolutely no reason at all. The reason may not be a good one, at least not in your view, but they will still have a reason. Think about it. Maybe they're worried they'll be in trouble, or perhaps they're jealous, or maybe they're very protective of their job or their kids or their property, or perhaps they're terrified of missing out on promotion with all their money problems, or they're hurt or feel ignored or want their contribution recognised. You may not know for sure, but you may be able to hazard a good guess. And that may help you to find a solution and with luck to feel at least a modicum of human empathy with them, even if you think their feelings are misplaced.

FEED IT
BACK

There's a technique known in business circles as feedback. It's a really useful way of letting people know how you feel without creating bad feeling. In other words, expressing yourself assertively rather than emotionally. It's especially useful when you have a persistent problem with someone; for example, they always dump work on you at the last minute so you have to stay late at work to get it done. Or they're always late when you arrange to meet up.

Tell the person how you feel. Don't start by saying, "You make me feel ..." Start with, "I feel ... when you ..." Decide in advance how you're going to say this. Avoid any emotive terms such as exaggeration, labelling, judging, criticism and so on. So you might say, "I feel frustrated when you give me work late in the day" (rather than, "You're so disorganised you're always late with everything and it ruins my evening"). Then explain why, for example, "I end up late home and then my evening is a rush to get everything done."

Now you have to give them a chance to respond, and you should show you're listening. Be prepared to quote instances if they ask, and be ready with a suggestion for solving the problem. For example, "Maybe we could have a cut-off time for giving me any work you want done that day." Then, of course, you have to hear them out and be prepared to compromise if need be. You should find this whole process straightforward and factual – and it will clear the air and help resolve the problem.

LEARN TO
DELEGATE

One of the most obvious ways to get things done is to get other people to do them for you. Whether it's family, team members or anyone else, it's a straightforward solution to at least some of your time problems. Some people find this easy, and others find it backfires. That's because you're not doing it right – sorry to be blunt, but there it is.

If you don't give the right job to the right person in the right way, it won't work. You need to choose someone who is capable of doing it – maybe they need a bit of training, in which case you'll need to provide that. Then you have to make sure they understand exactly what you want – the task, the standard, the time, the budget, and anything else that's important. And you need to give them responsibility so they can feel some pride in the job. So long as they meet your criteria (time, cost, standard and so on) you should let them do it their own way. Finally, you shouldn't just wander off and abandon them. Let them know you're there if they need you.

Once the job is done, they'll need thanks and praise if they've done it well, or why would they bother to make an effort for you next time? Sometimes you find this takes longer than doing the job yourself, of course. But so long as you can keep delegating similar tasks to this person, they'll get the hang of it and in the long run they'll save you plenty of time.

GET THE BEST
OUT OF PEOPLE

If the people around you are enthusiastic and willing, not only will they be more likely to help with your workload, they'll also try harder to avoid adding to it. So it's important to be able to get people on side if you're going to work smarter and make your life more relaxed.

The thing I've learned over the years, by watching people at work and at home, is that everyone is motivated by something different. Of course most people want recognition, praise and thanks, but some need it more than others. Once you've worked out what motivates a particular person, you can offer them the right incentive to work for you. This applies to family and friends just as much as work colleagues and team members.

Some people want status, some want money, others crave responsibility, or job satisfaction, or freedom, or a challenge, or recognition or thanks. Once you know what drives someone, you can exchange what they want for what you want.

Of course, on top of that, you need to be honest, straight, friendly, honourable and all those things (for more on that take a look at my book *The Rules of Life*). If people like and respect you, and you can offer them what they want, they'll do pretty much anything for you.[21]

---

[21] Apart from your own children, who always strike a harder deal than anyone else.

KNOW WHAT
REALLY
MATTERS

For me, my family come first without question. Then probably work. Then various other things from my social life to holidays and hobbies. I need to know this because when I have a lot to do it makes a difference to how much time I devote to tasks, how soon I get them done, and even whether they're far enough up the list on a busy day to get done at all.

Not only does this knowledge affect what I do, it also affects how I feel at the end of the day. There's never going to be a day when every task is complete and you have to go to bed because there's nothing else to do.[22] So you always look back over your day as a mix of things you got done and things you didn't. I hope this doesn't sound as if life is one long grind. You may have ticked off on your list such things as going to the movies, catching up with your best friend, opening your birthday presents, reading to your child, delivering a knock-your-socks-off presentation, and winning the pub football match.

That was still a to-do list. And a very pleasant one too. When you look back over it at bedtime, the only way to judge whether you did a good job is by seeing if the things that really mattered got done. For me, a day when I made it to the school play but didn't get my next chapter written would score a lot higher than the other way around. And I know this because I know what really matters. Make sure that you can do the same.

---

[22] Is there? If so, why are you reading this when you should be going out and getting a life?

Prioritise

If you have loads to do, and a risk that you might not get it all done – or not on time at any rate – it makes sense to be sure that the bits you do are the bits that most need doing. And how are you going to know what those are? Well, you could guess, I suppose, and you'd be right quite a lot of the time. But when you guessed wrong you could find yourself in deep water – something vital not done, things done in the wrong order so you don't have what you need, long-winded tasks taking up time you can't spare and so on.

The answer to all of this is to know what your priorities are. Suppose your car needs collecting from its MoT at the same time as your child's sports day? What if your boss has asked you to complete a report the same week you're taking part in a major squash tournament? Maybe you've got to pack to go on holiday, including loads of essentials to buy – from sun cream to mosquito repellent – and you still haven't arranged someone to call in and check on your elderly neighbour while you're away.

What order are you going to do these things in? Or can you get them all done? Or could you have avoided the problem if you'd seen this coming? (The answer to that one is yes.)

Having established what matters in life (on the previous page), you now need to use this information to establish what order to tackle your long list of tasks in.

KNOW WHAT IS URGENT
(AND WHAT ISN'T)

L ook, just because something is important, that doesn't mean it's urgent. It's vital that you recognise the difference if you're going to get things done as quickly and effectively as possible. Deciding which secondary school to apply to for your child in 6 months time is undoubtedly important. But is it urgent? Not by the sounds of it. You've still got 6 months before you need to apply. Meanwhile, buying more milk because you've just run out, or passing on an email address to a colleague, could be very urgent.

So separate tasks into important ones and urgent ones. Of course there may be an overlap, so think in terms of a matrix that looks like this.

	Urgent	Not urgent
Important	A	C
Not important	B	D

The first things to tackle each day are the tasks in the A box – both urgent and important. Then tackle B, then C and then D (this isn't complicated you see). Urgent tasks that aren't important need doing, but they shouldn't take up much of your time. After all, they're not important.

Organise your
to-do list

I hope by now that you've written down everything you have to do, somewhere. Try to get it all in one place, maybe in that notebook we were talking about earlier. If you have two *entirely* separate lists – one for work between 9 and 5 and one for everything else – that's fine. But if you tend to work at home or do personal stuff at work you really need one combined list.

Now you can decide what order to tackle it in. Do the urgent and important tasks first, and then quickly tick off the urgent only things. After that you need to use the information you have about what really matters (see page 140) and your list of priorities to work out roughly how to work through the rest of the list.

Put related groups of tasks (phone calls, or things to do while you're at the shops) together because this will be more steamlined, as we saw before. Now use the other list-making strategies we covered earlier to put these in order (you know, putting a few quick easy tasks at the top so you get lots of ticks quickly, that sort of thing).

If you've never done this before it may take a little while to sort out but it will save you oodles of time in the long run. Once you're in the habit it's even quicker because you'll write things down in the right place on the list from the off. If you've not been an organised person up to now, just try this and see how much more relaxed you feel when you have everything vital down in black and white, and you can see what you're supposed to be doing. It's almost a shame to start crossing things off your beautifully organised list.

Clear some
downtime

Your to-do list is great for organising all the things you have to do. But what about all the not-doing you want to fit into your life? Maybe you like having a breathing space to sit down with a cup of tea, or you want to take time out to chill with the kids, or you'd love to finish the book you're reading which has just got to an exciting bit.

All these things should be possible, but you need to put them on your list. They may not be tasks as such, but you can't schedule them in if they're not on the list. So make sure you give yourself blocks of time off from working through the list, because having a cup of tea, chilling with the kids and finishing your book matter too.

PLAN YOUR LIFE

It's a good idea to look ahead a bit. You know that if you go for a walk and never look up but just watch your feet all the time, you'll miss the best bits. And you're more likely to walk into a lamp post. Planning your life is no different.

So have a plan for the long term (such as start a family in a few years, or downshift to the country), and then have a plan for the year ahead. If you want to get promoted, move house, change jobs and so on, have an idea of when you want this to happen. Otherwise it will just drift. With a plan, you can see how you need to work towards it.

Similarly, you should have a slightly more detailed plan for the next 3 months, and a more detailed one still for this month. The way to do this is with a notebook, or whatever, in which you enter your plans for each month. So you don't have to write a fresh plan every few weeks – you just make sure that there's plenty of detail for the next month, a fair bit for the next 3 months and so on. Finally, you have a to-do list for this week and for today, which we've already looked at.

This isn't a diary of appointments – it's a long-term to-do list. That way you can always see where you're heading, and jot down anything that needs to be upgraded, from a vague ambition to something that will actually happen.

Don't just firefight

It's easy to spend all day every day dealing with things that get thrown at you – routine tasks, responding to requests, letters, emails, paying bills and so on. These are all things that will arrive on your doorstep if you sit there and do nothing.

However, most of the things that will really make you happy, such as the things on your plan for several months or years ahead, won't happen at all unless you go out and make them happen. Moving house, changing jobs, having kids, these are all things that require proactive work on your part.

You need to build time into your week for getting these vital things done, otherwise you're just firefighting all the time. If you don't make the time for these things, they'll never happen. The mail will get sorted, the school run will happen, the shopping and the bills will be dealt with, the filing will get done, but you'll still be here in 5 years with nothing to show for all the effort. If you want to be somewhere else in 5 years time, you need to do something about it.

HAVE A
THOROUGH
DIARY

W hat's in your diary? If it's just somewhere to write down appointments and meetings, you're not getting the most from it. Get yourself a bigger diary and start writing down everything that will end up on your to-do list that needs doing at a specific time.

Your diary should include phone calls you have to make, people you need to contact, letters to write and so on. If you need to book your train tickets next week, write a note in your diary to remind you. If you have to remember to return something you borrowed to your mate when you meet next week, write it down. Make a note of when the dog needs its flea treatment or your daughter has to take her recorder into school.

If you have software such as Outlook, that's even better. On one condition – you use it. If you have or can lay your hands on such a thing I heartily recommend you start using it because it's so easy to put recurring dates in, plus it reminds you of entries before they happen if you ask it to. So, instead of telling you it's your sister's birthday on the day, you can tell it to give you a couple of days' notice, which means you have time to sort out a card and post it.

I use Outlook myself and I'll tell you this – I worked out how to use it all by myself without any help and without resorting to the manual.[23] And I promise you, if I can understand it, it must be simple.

---

[23] I'm a bloke – I don't do 'instructions'.

KNOW WHAT
MAKES A
DIFFERENCE

There are times when you put something on your to-do list that frankly just isn't worth doing. You can be too conscientious. It was important to get your paperwork organised, but are you sure you really need to spend an hour colour-coding all the files? I know it will look organised and help you find things, but couldn't you have found them anyway?

And there are times when you don't have to do a job perfectly – good enough is, well, good enough. So you don't necessarily need to mark all your child's school uniform in two places. Just a marker pen on the washing label will probably do the job fine, without the iron-on tapes as well.[24] And you may think it looks impressive to give all those references at the end of your report, but will your boss really care? After all, if they want to know they can always ask.

Everything you do should make a worthwhile difference, otherwise you're just wasting your time. In an ideal world these things might be great, but you're pushed for time and you need to make sure that everything you spend your time on deserves your attention.

---

[24] You know they'll lose it anyway, whatever you do.

GET ORGANISED
AT WORK

You may be reading some of this thinking, "I don't need to do all that! I'm just struggling to get the shopping and the housework fitted round the kids." Well, it's your choice. If you're happy as you are, don't let me stop you.

However, if you have any kind of job, it's really important that you are organised and are seen to be organised. Your colleagues and your boss will judge you on how much you appear to get done, and the level of trust and responsibility you get at work, not to mention promotions and pay, will be heavily influenced by this perception.

So don't just *be* organised, *look* organised too. Don't say things like, "Now where did I put that? Honestly, I'd forget my head ..." or, "Someone rang for you. Hang on ... it will come back to me ...". Make sure that you look, sound and act organised and effective. That way you'll be trusted and relied on, and your boss will have you down as a safe pair of hands. That's got to count in your favour at the next salary review or job interview.

KNOW WHERE YOU'RE GOING

Quite apart from your to-do list, you need to have a broader picture of what you're trying to achieve. What do you want to have achieved by the end of the day? What will it take for you to look back this evening and think, "That was a good day"?

What you need is an objective. Maybe you're aiming to get the house looking presentable and all the shopping and everything you need for the weekend sorted. Maybe you want to complete the research for your proposal so you're ready to sit down and write it tomorrow. Maybe you want your afternoon meeting to agree the decision you're recommending. Maybe you want to organise your mother's garden and leave her feeling reassured and relaxed.

There may be more than one objective, but try to identify the key one or two. Not only does this help you stay on track through the day, focused on what's important, but it also means you'll feel better at the end of the day. If you've achieved your key objective, you can feel good even if a few minor things did get a bit lost along the way.

Know what
you're doing

Having set your objectives for the day, you now need to set your objectives for the key tasks you'll be working on. The question to ask yourself here is, "What would constitute a good result?"

If you're getting the house ready for the weekend, what's your reason? If it's just for your own peace of mind, what standard of tidiness does that require? If you have visitors, what standard do you consider that requires? Do you need to vacuum round the whole house? Tidy away all those piles of miscellaneous stuff about the place? Wash the kitchen floor? Or do you just want to look as if you've made an effort (squirt a bit of polish around so it smells clean)? If you don't know what your objective is, how can you know what needs doing?

And that proposal you're working on. How far through it do you want to be by the end of the day? And what standard of research are you aiming for? Do you need to be able to quote chapter and verse for every statement you make, or are you just aiming to collect a few general statistics to emphasise a couple of points? Again, unless you know what your objective is, you won't know what you're doing.

FIRST YOU MUST PUSH THE
WHEELBARROW AND THEN
YOU CAN SIT DOWN

This remark comes from a relative of mine who is autistic and lives in a home, where he works in their market garden. He has a delightfully straightforward way of looking at the world, and this is one of his regular expressions.

What he means, of course, and expresses so much better than most management advisers and the like, is that you need to set yourself targets and then give yourself a break when you reach them. You can treat yourself to a rest period as a reward, or you can just give yourself a break and switch to something else for a while. The important thing is that you know where you're aiming to get to and you'll make sure you don't stop until you reach it.

Don't work a week behind

You can deal with today's emails today. Or you can deal with last Wednesday's emails today. Which do you do? I used to be a week behind at least. Then someone pointed out to me that I was still having to stay on top of a day's worth of emails per day, whichever I did. It's just that one way made me look polite, efficient and organised, and the other way made me look uncivil, unorganised and less than competent.

So now I make sure I'm doing today's work and not last week's. My workload is no different, but now it looks better and I don't have that horrible sense of impending panic that it's all running away from me. Yes, of course there are days when everything gets on top of you and you just can't get to your inbox. I know that. But if you were up to date the day before, it won't take long to catch up.

The only tricky bit is clearing that backlog in the first place, but of course that's what your lists and plans are for. Or you could try a technique I discovered once, though I've never been able to bring myself to try it. I called a chap and said I'd emailed him last week, and he replied, "I was on holiday last week and when I got back I deleted everything in my inbox. There was too much to deal with." I asked him how he could be sure there wasn't anything important there and he told me, "There probably was. But if it's important they'll get back to me. You just have."

Don't do
things twice

If you want to get everything on your list done, for goodness sake don't try doing it more than once. There's no point reading your emails until you're going to deal with them – you'll only have to read them again when you come to reply. Sure, you can scan them to check there's nothing urgent, but that's it.

Likewise, don't sort through your mail and leave a pile of papers to deal with later. Deal with them now, or you'll just be repeating yourself. Did you know that, in a normal office, each piece of paper on someone's desk gets handled an average of seven times? Well, you haven't got time to do that. Pick it up, deal with it, put it down, end of story.

When you're tidying the house, don't pick something up, wonder what to do with it, and then put it down again because you can't decide. Don't deal with that stuff until you're ready to make a decision on it.

The only things you should be doing twice are the ones you both enjoy and have time for. Like mixing a gin and tonic in the evening, or kissing your partner.

DEAL WITH IT
WHEN IT HAPPENS

OK, so you've decided you're not going to operate a week's delay on dealing with your inbox, and you're not going to do things twice. You may be surprised how much time this is saving you. You've done brilliantly finding the time to catch up on your emails, and now you're wondering how you're going to keep up to speed and not slip behind again.

The way to do this is to make yourself a rule that you will deal with everything reactive when it happens. That email asking for a bit of information, or the cheque for the school trip ... all those little requests or jobs that only take a couple of minutes to do, get on with them and get them out of the way.

And, unless there's a good reason why you can't, you'll respond to each phone message or email or letter at your very next phone/email/letter session. Or you'll forward it or bin it if that's more appropriate.

Now, I find this one really tough. It's so tempting to put things on one side when I'm busy with something else. Of course, that's where I'm going wrong. But I've found it's true that, if you can just keep on top of them, they will never gang up together and grow into the nasty monster lurking on your conscience again.

ORGANISE
YOUR
SPACE

Oh no, here's another one I hate. And one of the reasons I hate it is because I know it's right and I don't want it to be.

If you keep your desk and your work area neat and tidy, you'll get more done. I know it's true. Think of all that time you'll save not rummaging for bits of paper (which you should have dealt with immediately of course) and trying to find your stapler.

I'm not naturally tidy. I have an infuriatingly neat friend who used to ask me to tidy up after myself when I visited his house. So I responded by asking him to untidy after himself when he visited me. "Please leave those crumbs where they are," I'd say. "And don't wash up your mug or pick up the magazines that got knocked on the floor." He hated it. Couldn't do it. Which proved my point, whatever it was – I don't recall exactly what the point was actually, but I felt it was proved anyway.

I hate being tidy. And I refuse to straighten piles of papers or files, or to colour-code everything. But even I have to admit, with deep reluctance, that I work more effectively when my desk isn't a mess, and related things are kept together.

Don't read things you don't need to[25]

[25] Or want to. I'm not including reading for pleasure in this.

Some jobs entail a vast amount of reading. Clearly if you're a proof-reader you're going to struggle to get out of this. But reading is very time-consuming and (if you're not a proof-reader) you can get away with doing a lot less of it than you might think. Do you honestly think your boss or your senior managers read everything in their in-tray word for word? What about government ministers with all those red boxes? Of course they don't read it all. They can't.

Start by checking the contents page. Which bits do you really need to read? If you're lucky the contents page may even tell you all you want to know. If you need to go further, look for the section or chapter summaries and just read those. Failing that, just read the closing paragraphs of the relevant sections. You may feel you need to read a few sections in full, but this will ensure you don't read anything unnecessary.

If you subscribe to trade magazines and newspapers, aim to read the top three articles in each and then just scan the headlines. Often the headline tells the whole story anyway.

If you have people working for you, you can always ask them to read books and reports and summarise them for you – insist the summary is no more than one side of paper.

It's largely a matter of attitude. If you think you ought to read everything, you'll feel guilty if you don't. But think in terms of your objective – aim to read the least you can in order to glean what you need to know. After all, extracting information is the only point of the exercise.

KEEP IT
TOGETHER

Keep everything you need for one task in the same place. I know it sounds obvious but it doesn't always happen like that. This might be electronic or it might be hard copy – what matters is that you always know where to find everything because there's only one folder it can be in.

This applies at home as well as work. Have a folder to keep instruction manuals and guarantees in, and another for everything to do with the car, and one for household bills and so on. It may seem like a pain but it's quick and easy to do, and you can save hours of time, not to mention loads of stress, searching for missing documents later.

MAKE SURE THE BOOMERANG COMES BACK

Why is it that people can't just do what they say they will? I mean, if they say they're going to put something in the post, how hard can it be to do it? This drives me mad, not least because when you've mentally put the ball in their court, you forget to deal with it yourself. You think you'll do it when the stuff arrives in the post, but of course, if they don't send it the thing falls off everyone's to-do list.

This is where some kind of diary is so useful. As soon as anything like this happens, and you're waiting on someone else to do something, make a note in your diary to chase them on Friday, or Tuesday week, or whenever you'd expect it to have happened by. I know it's not right or fair, and it certainly sticks in my craw when it's their fault if it doesn't happen, but the aim here is to get things done, not to allocate blame.

Just don't mentally put the ball in their court but see it as your job to chase until it happens, and make sure you've left yourself a reminder to do just that.

KEEP YOUR MEETINGS ON TIME

You know what the biggest time sapper at work is. If you work in a job where you have to go to meetings, they can devour time like nothing else. Think how much you'd get done if you never had to go to a meeting.

Of course meetings can be very worthwhile, but you don't want to waste unnecessary time. If you're chairing a meeting, make sure it starts on time and ends on time.

If people are late, start without them. And don't go back over everything when they arrive – tell them to read the minutes when they're circulated. That'll soon teach 'em. Once they learn that if they're late you won't wait for them, you'll pretty soon get a reputation for starting on time.

Now, how are you going to finish on time? You need to allocate time for each agenda item. Some will need time to discuss, but others can be dealt with quickly. However, they won't be unless you insist on it – boy, can some people waffle and get bogged down in detail and drag out meetings for hours. So keep pointing out that, "We've only got 3 minutes before we have to move on, so let's just establish who's going to do this and when they can report back. Fred – are you happy to take this on?" If each item runs on time, the whole meeting will finish on schedule. It's as simple as that.

Know what you're aiming for

If you've got to spend half an hour or half a morning in a meeting, at least let's make sure it's productive. After all, effective meetings can save you time and help get things done, so your time could be well spent.

If you're a small cog there may be little you can do, but if you're the big wheel and you're chairing the meeting, you can certainly make sure the meeting earns its keep. Make a note against every agenda item of what you want it to achieve. This will be one of three things (sometimes more than one):

- imparting information
- reaching a decision
- determining and allocating action.

You need to know before you hold the meeting what you're aiming for, otherwise you can end up having fruitless discussions and still come away having achieved nothing.

AVOID UNNECESSARY MEETINGS

If you work in an office, a huge amount of time can be taken up with meetings, getting in the way of everything else you have to do. A really good meeting is the best and quickest way to achieve results but, as you know, not all meetings are that good. Many of them waste time and achieve little.

If it's not compulsory to attend a particular meeting, think about whether you really need to go. Often we attend a meeting because it's there, when we could just as well skip it and read the minutes afterwards.

If you're calling a meeting, make sure you really need it to happen. The biggest culprits here are regular meetings. You hold them every Monday morning because ... that's what you do. Well, maybe some Mondays you don't need to. Or perhaps your weekly meeting could be fortnightly. Even if you just held it 3 weeks out of every 4, think of the time you'd free up for other things.

Don't get interrupted

You want to work effectively and get things done fast. It could make the difference between whether or not you get any lunch, or determine what time you get home and put your feet up this evening. So the last thing you want is interruptions. Right?

Well, there are lots of psychological ploys you can use here:

- For a start, close the door when you don't want to be interrupted, *but not otherwise*. If the door is always closed it means nothing.

- As soon as anyone pokes their head around the door say, "I'm really busy just now. Can you come back this afternoon/drop me an email/catch me at lunchtime?" The key here is to speak first – the longer you leave it the harder it gets.

- If anyone does come in, make sure they can't sit down because either you have no spare chair, or you keep it permanently covered in files.

- If you stand up that will signal the end of the conversation. Better still, never sit down in the first place.

- If the interrupter doesn't have enough to do and is just stopping for a chat, give them some work. That will deter them next time – "Hi Bob. Hey, could you just take this file down to Ali for me? I'm really busy."

Don't get
caught by
the phone

Personal interruptions are one thing. Now, how are we going to stop the phone disturbing you when you're busy? Here are some ideas for you:

- For a start, you can divert your phone or put it on voicemail. Just pick up messages during natural breaks in your workload.

- Or, as soon as you know who the caller is and before they've said anything but their name, you cut in with, "Hi Kate. I'm really busy at the moment. Can I call you back?" Then make sure you do call back of course.

- If you do answer, keep your responses to one or two words – it signals pretty quickly that you're in a hurry.

- Another option is to tell the caller what they want to know and then instantly hang up before they have time to respond, for example, "Yes, I've got the meeting in my diary for tomorrow so I can see you 5 minutes before it starts. Thanks, bye." Click.

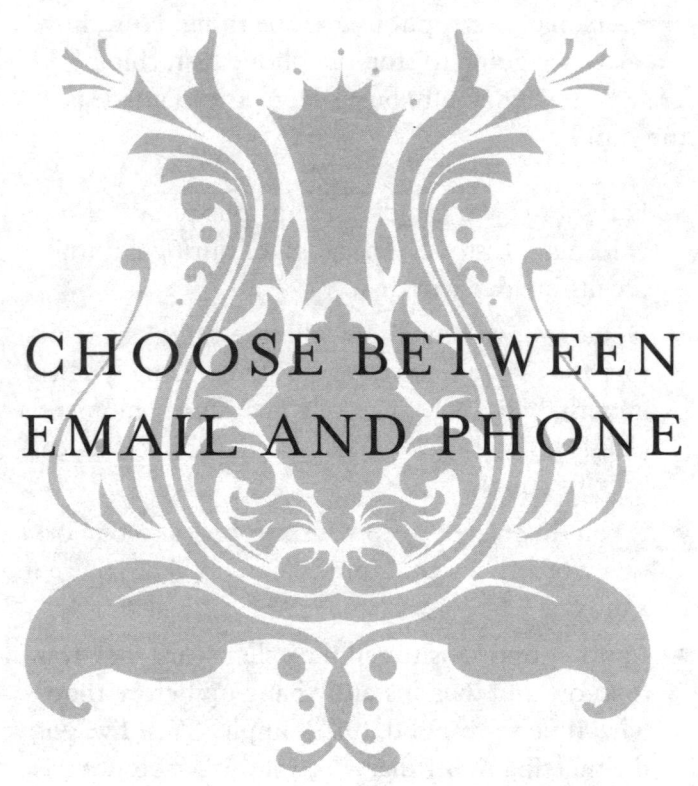

CHOOSE BETWEEN
EMAIL AND PHONE

If you want to save time, email beats the phone every time. But it's worth recognising what the phone is good for, so you can use it when it helps and make sure you avoid it the rest of the time. Here's why you might opt in favour of the phone:

- If you need to come to a quick joint decision it makes it easier to have a discussion.

- If there's any danger of feelings being hurt, toes being trodden on, ill-feeling being caused, dissent being sown or suspicion being generated, email can be misconstrued more easily, and is more likely to cause damage than a friendly phone call.

- Sometimes the matter for discussion is sensitive and you don't want to put it down in writing.

- It's harder to build a relationship by email. If this is someone you want to establish a bond with, and don't speak to in the normal way of things, it can help to pick up the phone once in a while and make real contact, and use email the rest of the time.

If none of these is the case, use email. It's much quicker.

Reduce
your inbox

Anything you can do to cut down on the number of emails in your inbox has to save you time. So make sure you have a good spam filter of some kind, and use it properly. Of course it won't get rid of all the spam, but it will cut it right down.

Apart from the emails you're supposed to get – whether you want them or not – the other big time sapper is personal 'junk' emails. You know, round robins and the like. There are two options here (you can combine them if you like). If you want these emails, but not when you're at work, have two email addresses, one work and one personal. Make sure everyone in your address book knows which one to use. Then check your personal emails during leisure time.

The alternative is to email everyone in your address book (apart from your boss and your customers) saying, "My email address is for work and it is taking me too long to go through it each day. So please could you stop sending me any round robins, jokes, chain letters, petitions to sign, gossip, charity requests and anything else that isn't work related. Thank you."

DITCH
THE PING

It's hard to see it when it's happening, but you lose a huge amount of time switching tasks. They call it 'pick up and set down time' and it describes the extra time you spend starting a task – getting things together and getting your head round what you're doing – and the time you spend saving it or filing it or putting it away. If you keep coming back to a task throughout the day, you're wasting all these little bits of time when you could have just ploughed through it in one go.

And what interrupts most of us during the working day more than anything else? Emails, that's what. That little ping that lets you know a new email has arrived, and you just have to go and have a peek, don't you? Just in case it's something interesting, or that reply you were waiting for, or a piece of good news.

Look, the whole point about email is that it sits there until you're ready to pick it up. That's where it scores over, say, a phone call. The sender knows that if you don't check your inbox until tomorrow, there it will be. So there's no earthly point checking it every two minutes.

Aim to check your inbox three times a day – when you start work, after lunch, and at the end of the day. Ditch the junk and deal with anything pressing the first two times, and try to get rid of everything you can the last time. One of the advantages of this is that you can schedule in time for this, whereas it's hard to plan for a couple of minutes every time you hear a ping.

STOP PLAYING
GAMES

Right, that's enough, stop it. Go into your computer and take all those games off it right now. Whether it's solitaire, free cell or anything else, they're the enemy of good organisation and getting things done.

GET IT OVER WITH

If you want to get through meetings and phone calls faster – at home or at work – don't sit down. The psychological effect of sitting in a chair makes you feel you're in for a long haul. It's easy to stand on the phone, and it encourages you to see it as a swift exchange of information rather than a social chat.

You might feel a bit of a prat if you're the only one standing up through the meeting, but don't forget that everyone else there has a to-do list about the size of yours, and they don't want to waste time either. So suggest to everyone that you hold the meeting on your feet. It imparts a satisfying sense of urgency. Obviously this won't work during a two-day conference, but it's great for team meetings and project meetings.

DON'T GIVE UP

If your life is a permanent rush to get everything done, it's not going to change to a life of calm relaxation by waving a magic wand.

It will take you time to incorporate new strategies into your life that make you more effective. So don't feel you can't do this if you haven't managed to free up loads of time in the first few days. You can't get into too many new habits at once.

Pick out the things you think will make most difference, and once they're integrated into your life add a few more, and then a few more. Within days you'll start to notice a difference, and within weeks there'll be a major change.

Everyone can get more done if they decide to make it happen, and that includes you. Stick with it, and you'll find that not only are you achieving far more, you're also making less effort and your life is more relaxed. And who can argue with that?